THE CENTAUR
&
THE BACCHANTE

THE CENTAUR
&
THE BACCHANTE

Maurice de Guérin

Translated & with an afterword
by Gian Lombardo

Quale Press

Translation from the French text of Maurice de Guérin's
"Le centaur" and "La bacchante," and afterword
copyright © by Gian Lombardo

"The Centaur" previously appeared in *Beginnings of the Prose
Poem — All Over the Place*, Mary Ann Caws &
Michel Delville, eds. (Black Widow Press, 2021).

Cover: *Main face of sarcophagus: Dionysos and Ariadne drawn
by centaurs*, ca. 230–235 BCE. After restoration. Roman.
870 x 217 cm. Photo by Hervé Lewandowski, Musée du
Louvre, Paris, France. Used by permission RMN-Grand
Palais/Art Resource.

ISBN: 978–1–935835–27–1 trade paperback edition

LCCN: 2021942056

Quale Press
www.quale.com

CONTENTS

THE CENTAUR

I WAS BORN IN THESE MOUNTAIN CAVES. The first moments of my life trickled into the shadows of my secluded abode without disturbing the silence, just like this valley's river whose first drops fall from some weeping rock in a remote cavern. When our mothers near giving birth, they wander into those caverns, and in their furthest, most untamed recesses, in the dankest shadows, they drop, without issuing even a moan, fruit as taciturn as themselves. Their potent milk enables us to overcome whatever struggles such infants might have to endure without succumbing. Yet we leave our caves later than you leave your cradles. It's common knowledge among us that we need to withdraw from the world and safeguard our first stage of existence as days when we commune solely with the gods. My growth charted its own course almost entirely in the shadows where I had been born. The location of my abode was struck so deep into the mountain that I would never have known an exit

existed if the winds, after turning and
twisting so many times from that dis-
tant opening, had not sometimes cast
me a sudden draught of freshness or
storminess. Sometimes, too, my moth-
er returned, swathed in scents from the
valleys or drenched and dripping from
the waters into which she often dove.
However, when she returned, she never
told me about those little valleys or
their streams. Rather, I inhaled what
emanated from her — which upset me
— and I paced this way and that in the
darkness. What, I asked myself, is this
realm outside that has so much power
over my mother? What reigns there that
is so compelling that it so frequently
beckons her? What's so unsettling out

there that she comes home each time in such a different mood? Sometimes my mother would come back animated with a profound joy. Sometimes she'd be so sad, shuffling her feet or limping along. Even from a distance I could detect her good spirits in how she carried herself and directed her gaze. I felt her moods with every fiber of my being. But her anguish seized me most strongly and ensnared me much more deeply into convoluted conjectures. In those moments, I worried about my own fortitude, recognizing that I possessed a force that could not be contained. It took hold of me, making me thrash my arms about or redouble my strides in the broad shadows of the cave. I started to realize — through the blows that I struck in the void and the frenzied steps I made there — what my arms must embrace and where my feet must bring me... Ever since, I have wrapped my arms around the torsos of centaurs, the bodies of heroes and the trunks of oaks. My hands have touched rocks, waters, innumerable plants and cupped the most subtle impressions of the air. I lift them up during impenetrable and serene nights to intercept the breezes and then glean from them signs to guide my way. Look, Melampus, how worn my hooves are! And yet, as stiff as I am in the far reaches of old age, there are still days when, in broad daylight on mountain summits, waving my arms

7

and summoning all the speed left in me, I bolt as I did in my youth — and for the same reasons.

These fits alternated with long absences with no frantic movement. During those times I no longer possessed any other feeling in my whole being than that of maturation, which little by little welled in me. Having lost my taste for those outbursts, and having withdrawn into an absolute peace, I tasted without adulteration the benevolence of the gods who surged within me. Calm and shadow governed my thirst for life's secret allure. Shadows who inhabit these mountain caverns, I owe to your silent care the mystic education that so tenaciously nourished me.

Shadows, under your watch I have tasted
life as pure as it can be — life as it ema-
nated from the very heart of the gods!
When I descended from your sanctuary
into the light of day, I staggered and did
not greet the light because it seized me
so violently, drugging me as if it were
a fatal potion suddenly coursing in my
veins. I warrant that my being, until
then so stable and uncomplicated, shud-
dered and lost much of itself as if leaves
blown in the wind.

O Melampus, why do you want to
learn about the lives of the centaurs?
Which god's will guided you to me,
the oldest and saddest of them all? It
has been a long time since I practiced
anything of their ways any more. I never

leave this mountain top where old age has confined me. These days, I use my arrows only to uproot stubborn plants. Placid lakes still recognize me but rivers have forgotten me. Yet I will tell you some things about my youth. But, beware, those recollections issue from a corrupt memory and sputter like a stingy libation trickling from a leaky pitcher. I have recounted my infancy without difficulty because it was tranquil and perfect. Life pure and simple filled me — it's easy to retain and retell those memories without sorrow. O Melampus, if a god were begged to recount his life, he would utter just a few words!

So full of commotion, my youth passed quickly. I lived to move and my steps knew no bounds. Proud of my free-roaming, I wandered through every part of this wilderness. One day as I followed a gorge rarely visited by centaurs, I discovered a man who was skirting the river on the opposite bank. He was the first human that I had ever seen. I sneered at him. There, at most, I said to myself, goes only half of me! Look how minced his steps are and how awkwardly he carries himself! His eyes seem to measure space with sadness. Undoubtedly, he must be some centaur undone by the gods and reduced to scurrying like that.

In my forays I often spent much of my time refreshing myself by wading in river beds. Half of me would be hidden under water, struggling to keep upright so the other half would appear unruffled as I strode with my arms folded above the torrent. I lost myself thus among those waves, succumbing to their divagations that took me far and wide, which conveyed all the beauty of the riverbanks to their savage guest. How many times, surprised by nightfall, I floated along the current under lengthening shadows spreading the gods' nightly influence to the furthest reaches of the valleys! My impetuous life tempered then to the scantiest remnant of a single subtle feeling of existence diffused equally throughout my entire being, like the shimmering gleams of the goddess who traverses the nights in the waters where I swam. Melampus, my dotage makes me miss the rivers. The majority peaceful and monotonous, they accept their destinies more calmly than centaurs, and with a more constructive wisdom than men. When I left them, I was attended by their gifts that accompanied me day in and day out, and that dissipated only slowly, like all perfumes do.

A wild and blind inconstancy took hold of my steps. In the middle of the most furious headlong dash, it sometimes occurred to me to break my stride suddenly, as if an abyss had opened up at my feet or a god blocked my path. These sudden stops fueled my fits even more. Sometimes I cut branches in the forests and brandished them over my head as I ran. So fast did I run their leaves bent with barely a flutter but when I slowed and stopped, wind and movement returned to them, and they murmured and rustled again. Thus my life flickered in my very core except when I would suddenly erupt with one of my impetuous dashes through these valleys. I listened to my being's roiling flood, listened to it as it fed the flames that it had fanned in the expanse that I had just madly crossed. My quivering flanks struggled against the onrush that pressed inward on them, and tasted pleasure in the upheaval, known only to seashores, to corral without diminishment a fevered and excitable life.

Meanwhile, with my head cocked to catch the wind's freshness, I observed how quickly the summits of the mountains had become so far away, as well as the tree-lined riverbanks and their waters — waters that followed a lazy course, and trees firmly rooted in the earth, with only their branches moving in the gusts of wind that made them groan. "I alone," I said to myself, "am free to move. I have lived my life from one end of these valleys to the other. I am happier than the torrents that cascade from the mountains never to return to their source. The sound of my steps is more beautiful than the creak of branches and rush of wave. That sound is the reverberation of a

15

wandering centaur who has no guide but himself." So while my sweating flanks were drunk with my flight, I felt my pride surge and, turning my head, I paused for a while to behold my steaming croup.

Youth is like a verdant forest besieged by gales: it stirs up from every which way life's abundant gifts, always letting some haunting murmur reign in the foliage. Living amid the rivers' abandon, inhaling Cybele unceasingly, either in the river beds or on the peaks, I bounded everywhere, living carefree and unfettered. When night, filled with a divine calm, found me on the slopes and led me to some caves' openings, it was there that I was pacified in the same way night stills the sea, letting abide in me those delicate undulations that forestall sleep without disturbing rest. Stretched out on the threshold of my retreat, my hindquarters hidden in the cave and my head under the sky, I watched the parade of shadows. Then those strange happenings that had so amazed me during the day escaped drop by drop, returning to Cybele's peaceful heart just as after a heavy rain the remaining drops clinging to the leaves fall and rejoin the waters below. It is said that during the night the sea gods abandon their palaces deep under the water's surface and, sitting upon headlands, they gaze upon the ocean's expanse. In like manner I kept watch, having at my feet a vast panorama of life similar to those gods' sleeping sea. Returned to a full and clear consciousness, I felt as if I had just been born, as if the core of the watery abyss that had conceived me left me high and dry on the top of the mountain, like Amphitrite's waves stranding a dolphin on the strand at low tide.

My gaze ranged widely and I espied even the most distant points. Like footprints on a sand bar, the western ridge of mountains retained impressions of sunset scintillations that darkness could not erase. Naked and pure summits persisted in pale clarity. I sometimes saw Pan descend there, always alone. Sometimes I also heard a choir of Orphic gods, or saw some mountain nymph pass by enraptured with night. Sometimes eagles from Mount Olympus flew to the heavens and vanished into distant constellations or roosted in sacred groves. The spirit of the gods, bestirring themselves, suddenly shattered the ancient oaks' tranquility.

Melampus, you seek wisdom, which is the science of the gods' will. You wander among your kind, a mortal waylaid by destiny. In this land, there's a stone that, when touched, issues a sound similar to that of an instrument's string breaking. It has been said that Apollo, who tended his sheep in this wilderness, placed his lyre on that stone, abandoning its melody there. O

Melampus, wandering gods set their lyres on stones but no one... none forgot one there. During the time when I kept watch in the caves, I sometimes believed that I was going to surprise the dreams of a sleeping Cybele, and that the mother of gods, betrayed by her dreams, would part with some of her secrets in her sleep. Yet I never discovered any sound save what dissolved in night's whispers or dissolved in the indistinct words from raging rivers.

"O Macareus," one day great Chiron, whom I cared for in his old age, said to me, "we are both centaurs of the mountains but our temperaments are so different! You see, I directed all of my attention to the study of plants. You, on the other hand, you are like those mortals who collect water or firewood or bring to their lips some pieces of Pan's broken reedpipe. Consequently, those mortals, having inhaled what remains of a god's breath from those pipes, become possessed by a wild spirit or perhaps erupt in some strange frenzy. Restless and seized by an unknown purpose, they set out into the wilderness, plunge themselves into the forests, skirt waterways, become one with the mountains. Mares beloved by winds in distant Scythia are neither wilder than you nor sadder in the evening after the North Wind has died down. Do you want to know the gods, Macareus? Do you want to know from

21

whence men, animals and the principles of universal fire come? Ancient Ocean, father of all, keeps these things secret to himself. His attendant nymphs describe a choir circling around him and constantly sing to drown out anything that might escape from his lips during sleep. Mortals who touched the gods because they were virtuous received lyres from them to delight whomever might hear them, or novel seeds that enrich them — but nothing from the gods' unyielding mouths.

"In my youth, Apollo disposed me towards plants, and taught me how to extract beneficial sap from their veins. Since then, I have steadfastly confined myself to the great abode of these mountains, unsettled, unceasingly occupying myself in the search for simples, and in communicating the healing properties that I discover. Do you see from here the bald peak of Mount Oeta? Alcide laid it bare to build his funeral pyre. O Macareus! the demigod children of the gods heap lion skins on their pyres and are consumed on desolate mountaintops! The poisons of the earth taint blood derived from the immortal ones! And we centaurs, begotten by a reckless mortal paired with a goddess clothed as a cloud, what aid could we ever hope for from Jupiter who struck down the father of our race? The gods' vulture eternally rends the entrails of the artisan who shaped the first man. O Macareus! men and centaurs acknowledge as authors of their blood those who stole the privilege from the immortals. Perhaps whatever is beyond them is only what has been robbed from them, what is only the slightest mote of their essence dispersed far and wide, as if it were a flitting seed borne on the all-powerful wind of destiny. It is well known that Aegeus, father of Theseus, hid keepsakes and proofs under a rock by the sea with which his son could one day recognize his birth. The jealous gods have hidden somewhere testimony of the origin of everything, but at the edge of what ocean did they roll the stone that covers that evidence, O Macareus!"

Such was the wisdom great Chiron conveyed to me. Reduced to the last reaches of old age, that centaur nourished the noblest discourse in his spirit. His still robust body scarcely deviated from the straight by only the slightest pitch, as if he were an oak tree beset by wind. The force of his steps hardly suffered from age's debits. It could be said that he retained vestiges of the immortality he once received from Apollo but that had since been rendered back to that god.

As for myself, Melampus, I wither into decrepitude, tranquil as the setting constellations. Yet I still retain enough headstrongness to clamber onto rocks where I'll then loiter, either to survey the wild and restless clouds, or to watch the weepy Hyades, the Pleiades or bright Orion rise from the horizon. I know that I am fading, quickly melting away like a snowflake landing on water. Soon I will mingle with the rivers that flow into the deepest reaches of the earth.

THE BACCHANTE

THERE'S THE BALD MOUNTAIN RANGE where choruses roamed all along its peaks. Priestesses, torches, divine sounds have receded into its valleys. The celebration has vanished. Mysteries have retreated into the hearts of the gods. I am the youngest of the Bacchantes who grew up on Mount

29

Cithaeron. The choruses had not yet borne me to those summits because the sacred rites had barred me due to my youth. They ordered me to put in my time before entering into their solemn acts. In due time, the Hours, those arcane nursemaids who took great pains to make us fit for the gods, situated me among the Bacchantes, and I emerge now from those initial mysteries that swaddled me.

Before I attained the age required to practice the rites, I was like the young fishermen who live along the seacoast. They sometimes appear atop a rock, body bent and arms extended towards the water, like gods ready to dive back into the sea, but their souls hesitate in their mortal breasts and hold them back. Finally they do jump and some of them, it's said, reappear anointed on the waves. Thus I remained for a long time, on the verge of leaping into the mysteries. I abandoned myself at last to them and my head resurfaced thus anointed and dripping wet.

Bacchus — eternal youth, intense and omnipresent — early on I recognized your signs within me and summoned all my energy in order to devote myself to your divinity. One day, I walked toward the rising sun during the season when that god's rays fill ripening fruit and add the final touches to the labors of the earth. I went off into the hills in order to offer myself to his presence, to loosen my tresses before him at the first sign of light upon the horizon because one knows that hair inundated with morning flames becomes more luxurious and also becomes endowed with a beauty equal to Diana's. Going outside, my eyes caught the edges of shadows diving back under Earth's axis. Some celestial configurations, slowly finishing their descent towards the waves, still etched the nearly vacant sky. And the silence left by night lingered in the clearings. But just as it happens in the cool valleys of Thessaly, the rivers have the habit of shedding a mist similar to clouds, and which rests on them like the essence of your breath, O Bacchus, which was exhaled on the earth's breast during darkness and reigned upon the sun's return across the great, wide expanse of land. I enter those domains with life coursing in my breast as powerful and splendiferous as the pallidly rising constellations that shed a portion of their brightness to defeat night's abyss. When I paused climbing up the highest of the hills, I staggered like the priests who lift the gods' statue with their arms onto its sacred pedestal. My heart, having gathered the essence of the god scattered throughout that realm, understood the disorder that drove my steps and troubled my thoughts like waves rendered mad by the winds. No doubt, O Bacchus, this was at the behest of the disturbance that you poured into my heart, for the gods surprise the spirits of mortals in this way, like the sun that, eager to penetrate nearby branches thick with shadows, sends the North Wind to rustle them open.

Then Aëllo turned up. That Bacchante — daughter of Typhon, the most impetuous of all the winds, and from a mother who wandered among the mountains of Thrace — had been raised by the nymphs of those lands, deep in caverns far from men. For the gods place their trust in rivers that meander into the great desolate regions, or trust in nymphs who live in the least accessible places in the forest to care for the children issued from the gods' unions with the daughters of the elements or with mortals. Aëllo came from Scythia where she had scaled the crests of the Riphaen mountains, and journeyed through Greece, stirring up the mysteries everywhere and bringing their clamor high into the mountains. She reached the age when the gods, like the shepherds who divert water from the meadows, close off the flows that water the youth of mortals. Although she prided herself on living a completely full life, she had to admit its edges were starting to shrivel. Besides, her practice of the mysteries had taken its toll on the essence of her beauty, which exhibited clear signs of waning. Her hair, as thick as Night's, fell about her shoulders, attesting to the strength and richness of the gifts she received from the gods. But maybe she had let her hair down too many times in the whirl of Hyperborean winds or maybe she was seized by some unknown fate, but her hair had greyed, suffering far ahead of time the abuse of accumulated years. Her gaze still commanded an empire of the vastest stretch of lands and the furthest reaches of the sky. Her gaze moved consciously and steadily, aimed by preference toward the shores of heaven where divine shadows play — shadows that receive deep within them everything that vanishes over the horizon. Meanwhile, this grand and encompassing gaze off

and on became troubled and driven
into confusion, like an eagle's sight
at the moment when its eyes sense
the earliest traces of night. She also
demonstrated uncertainty in how she
carried herself. Sometimes she would
glory in her steady and easy saunter as
she walked along streams or through
forests. And sometimes her gait was
halting, like Leto looking near and
far for a place of refuge to give birth
to the gods she conceived. Sometimes
the hesitation of her steps and the
lowering of her head, which seemed
pained and heavy, would make you
think she was walking on the ocean's
floor. When night lulled her heart into
a ubiquitous calm, her majestic and

exceptionally clear voice rang out in the dark like the song the Hesperides sing where the seas end.

Aëllo befriended me and carefully taught me what the gods do when around mortals chosen to receive their favor, and who they themselves want to rear. Like the young Arcadians who descend with the god Pan to the most secluded forests in order to learn from him how to place their fingers on his wild pipes, and also to record in their minds the plaintive cry of the reeds, I went about with the grand Bacchante who, every day, directed her steps towards some remote spot. It was in these abandoned places that she felt comfortable speaking, and I listened to her words wend their way as if I had discovered the hidden source of a river.

"The nymphs who reign in the forests," she said, "enjoy stirring perfumes or songs so sweet along the edges of the woods that passersby lose their way and find themselves ending up at the darkest of forbidding places. A subtle effect pervades a stranger's spirit, confusion roils in them undermining the steadiness of their steps and, when they advance like those rural demigods who always carry forth with some sort of drunkenness in their veins, the nymphs take pride in the power they maintain over the minds of mortals.

"But Bacchus makes everyone who breathes feel the intoxication of his breath — even the illustrious family of gods. His breath, always regenerating, covers the whole earth, nourishes the eternal drunkenness of the furthest reaches of the Ocean and, driven into the divine air, churns the stars that constantly rotate around the dark pole. When Saturn, under night's mantle, mutilated sleeping Uranus, the land and the sea received a new lushness from the spilt blood whose first fruits were nymphs on land and Aphrodite from the seas. Bacchus ceaselessly kept a temperate plume pulsing within Cybele's humid chest, sustaining the warmth of old blood that still begets whole choirs of nymphs in dense forests and in immortal sea foam.

"Rivers have their homes in the deep palaces of the earth, in vast and resounding residences where those gods who bend down from up on high preside over the birth of springs and the headwaters of streams. They rule, their ears continually fed with a surfeit of babbling, and their eyes are fixed on the fate of their waves. But neither the scale nor the impenetrable state of their vaults can shield these divinities from Bacchus because the forces of fate did not prohibit him access. Rivers toss and turn in their beds and ancient silt swirls in the interiors of their clouded eddies.

"Through one summer's reign I made my abode on the summit of

Mount Pangea. The secret attractions I recognize each year, the joys of the earth and the beauty of the nearby countryside spurred me to take to the mountains' steep slopes. Mortals favored by the gods or who have been touched by an excess of misfortune have been led up high above and taken their place among the celestial signs: Maia, Cassiopeia, the great Chiron, Cynosouros and the sad Hyades have entered the silent parade of constellations. Guided by the forces of fate, they climb into the heavens, and set without deviation or surprise. Doubtless this rising and setting parade ever continues, initiates an ecstatic state with unknown bounds, cadging sameness from its

routes lined liberally with opium pop-
pies. I preferred just to stroll slowly up
the steep mountain slopes. It begat in
me a state of consciousness parallel to
what the stars exhibit in their routes
across the sky. I scale my road to the
mountain heights the same way stars
rise by degrees through the night. But
fruit cannot avoid becoming ripe. Every
day the earth insists on giving us more
pressing gifts whose consuming fire
burnishes skin with richer and richer
hues. Similarly struck and with my heart
conquered, I was powerless to reject or
avoid the life offered to me. Drugged
steps, seeking sanctuary in these for-
ests sacred to these silent divinities and
so potently lulled, were made drows-

ier by acute pain's sorrow. There were long hiatuses under the influence of breezes stirring at dusk, the sun's setting having occurred. Neither the empty night shadows nor dreams could stay for a moment the secret longings from which my mind suffered. I came upon the mountain heights that received the footprints of the immortals because some among them like to travel this stretch of mountains, holding fast to their unremitting trek along the undulating ridges, while others, on the crags that dominate in the distance, pass the time plunging into the recesses of the valleys, noticing the first signs of night or reflecting on how shadows and dreams control mortals' minds.

At these heights, I clutched at night's gifts, the peace and sleep that quell even the restlessness aroused by the gods. But that peace was similar to that of birds, friends of the winds and ceaselessly borne on their currents. When they obey the shadows and burst into flight toward the forests, their feet alight on branches that pierce the sky and are easily brushed by the breezes that traverse the night. They rejoice in the winds' buffeting even asleep and want their feathers to ruffle and open at the slightest breeze wafting across the forest canopy. Thus, deep in sleep, my spirit remained exposed to Bacchus's breath. This breath overtakes us by spreading in an ever-widening wave and is communicated to everything that loves light. However, a small number of mortals, privileged by the forces of fate, know how to keep themselves informed about where it blows. It presides all the way up to the highest peak of Olympus, and even touches the heart of the gods protected by the aegis or dressed in invincible tunics. It reverberates constantly around Cybele, and guides the tongues of the Muses who weave into their songs the unabridged story of the generation of gods holed up in the bowels of the earth, in the darkest part of boundless night, or in the Ocean that harbored so many immortals.

"Upon waking from sleep, I yielded my steps to the handiwork of the Hours. They guided my course throughout the day, and I roamed the mountain, driven by the sun, like the shadows that whirl around the base of the oaks. Gods halted the steps of a few mortals lingering at the waters, in the dark reaches of the forests or on the slopes of the hills. Suddenly their feet dug into the ground like roots, and all the life they contained flooded into branches and shot forth in leaves. Some, clinging to the edge of still waters, preserve a sacred tranquility and welcome at the break of day a host of dreams that take refuge in their shadowy branches. Others, growing in Jupiter's groves or towering on the bare fruitless summits, carry old and wild crowns buffeted by every wind, and are always beset by some of those wayward birds on which mortals forge prophesy. Their fate is immutable because the divine earth possesses them and they are eternally required to take nourishment from its heart. Even though they've been made whole, in the stillness of their being they yet retain some faint stirrings of their prior state. Whether the seasons wax or wane, they remain dependent on the sun. Of everything that moves in the universe, they only detect its rays, and it's to the sun alone who they convey what confused wishes they can still form. Such is the strength of their affection some of them even draw their

growth's direction from the march of
the gods and turn the fullness of their
branches towards his path. Along my
own path, upon which I entered fol-
lowing daybreak, I saw my pace slack-
en as I persevered, even though my
reserves were still full, and fizzle finally
into total collapse. Then I became like
those mortals woven into bark and
anchored onto the earth's potent core.
Held in abeyance, I received life from
the passing gods, without budging and
with arms extended toward the sun.
It was around the time of day when
the sun possesses its most stunning
brightness. Everything stopped on the
mountain, the endless forest no longer
exhaled, the fecund rays illuminated

Cybele, and Bacchus intoxicated every-
thing down to the foundations of the
islands in the deepest reaches of the
Ocean.

"The course of the setting sun
guided my way towards the mountain's
most distant Western reaches. The
god vanished and the light left behind
exhibited a crude admixture with
shadow. The depth of the valleys and
the entire breadth of the countryside
regained very slowly the freedom to
breathe. Birds flew above the trees, see-
ing if the flow of the winds in the sky
had been reestablished but their wings
were still intoxicated and barely sus-
tained an unsteady and erratic flight.
A rustling borne on the forest canopy

testified to the awakening of the breez-
es, but the tree tops only slightly trem-
bled, which did not compare to the
turbulence experienced by the cypress
branches in Pan's hands when the god
retreats from the choruses that he con-
ducts throughout heaven-sent nights:
the impassioned rhythm clings to his
steps and makes him reel unsteadily
among the sleeping trees. Wild ani-
mals exited from their dens to scale
heights and breathe more fiercely: their
eyes flashed anew, their terrifying cries
faded into murmurs and their bold gait
cobbled into listless staggering.

"Meanwhile, shadows filled the
depths of the valleys. They rose before
me distributing sleep and dreams to

everything that breathes. In the end, they approached me and enveloped me, but did not conquer me. I remained strong and alert under the weight of the night, while the earth, laden with sleep, quieted my limbs and reduced them to a general stillness. I stood watch without being seized with tiredness. I was enlivened with all the gifts the gods disseminated during the day. Their charm surrounded me and the new life that I had acquired sent its fiery spirits coursing through me.

"Callisto, clothed in a savage form through Juno's jealousy, wandered for a long time the earth's inhospitable places. But Jupiter, who loved her, stole her from the woods in order to include her

among the stars and led her fortunes
into a tranquility from which they can-
not deviate. She found her home at the
bottom of the tenebrous sky that dis-
persed the elements, gods and mortals
throughout Cybele's womb. The sky
arrays around her its most ancient shad-
ows and causes her to breathe what still
remains of the principles of life, joining
there the waves of relentless fire whose
emanations drive the universe. Drenched
with an eternal intoxication, Callisto
keeps spinning about the axis while the
whole order of the constellations passes
and sinks into the Ocean. So, during
the night, I keep still atop the mountain
ridge, my head swathed in a drunken-
ness that pressed upon it like the crown

of vines and fruit that sustains eternal youth on Bacchus's brow."

Thus Aëllo taught me by recounting her life. Once dedicating myself to following the voice that had called it to the knowledge of the gods, my mind was no longer swayed by the multitudes where it had its first home: it made its way towards the less frequented mysteries. Every day the word of the grand Bacchante rose before me, carrying me along the esotericism of her way. Often the Muses take leave of the choruses's rapid clip in order to begin walking at a slow pace into the heart of the night. Clad in the thickest of clouds and heading into the most distant mountains, they let loose divine songs amid the shadows. Aëllo's speech led me toward the gods forging ahead in the same way the Muses's voices wafted through the dark. A cave overlooking the plains, summits that capture the last traces of daylight, floors of the most fertile valleys — such were the places where the force of Aëllo's will guided me. Her homilies quite often lasted long into the depths of the night, and then she withdrew alone, letting her words cling in my mind like nymphs who, tying their wet clothes on low-hanging branches, return to their mysterious dwelling places.

Meanwhile, the mysteries were approaching that would finally sweep

me away with them, but they first
stirred in the Bacchantes long before
the hour when they arise. Each of
us, having recognized in ourselves
the signs the god placed on us, began
from that time to wander away because
mortals affected by the deities imme-
diately cover their tracks and head for
new climes. Each of us were inclined
to go wherever our wills led us. These
predelictions propelled us through-
out every quarter of the countryside,
like the nymphs, daughters of Heaven
and Earth, who, from their birth, scat-
ter from the mouths of springs, from
various sections of the forests and all
the places where Cybele had amassed
evidence of her fertility. We accepted

the fate of the gods who set out to rule the elements. They rejoiced in regarding the life that spreads out under their gaze, exerting power over the rivers and the fertile valleys. But throughout this careful leisure that they lead, their immortal life conforms to the same ebb and flow of waves and their nature is engaged by the elements they survey, like a man overtaken at riverbanks by sleep and dreams, and whose robe falls into the flow. Each Bacchante is thus aligned with some place marked by the birth of an innate fate. Aëllo appeared on the hilltops and for a long time rested her head on Earth's breast. She seemed to be waiting, like Melampus, son of Amphythaon, for a snake with markings resembling a poppy to come slither around her temples. Hippothea, seated where the springs bubble forth, was rendered motionless there. Her hair, all undone, her arms slack and her gaze fixed on the flow of the waters bore witness to following their destiny and for her thoughts to be one with the flow. Plexaure's route plunges into the broadest forests. When an Oceanid is overtaken by sleep as she travels the seas, her limbs give way and she falls on the current as if on a bed. She relinquishes the direction of her journey to the whim of the waves. Floating (one would say from afar a mortal had died), she is spread with the softness of life on the wave that sweeps her away and her heart takes on a sleep instilled by the Ocean. Plexaure asleep on her forest bed appears likewise. Stopped at the edge of a steep precipice, Telesto leaned over, thrusting her arms toward the valleys, like Ceres on Etna's summit, where the goddess, advancing across the opening of the crater, lights her pine torch in the volcano's fire.

As for me, who was still unacquainted with the god, I ran wildly through the countryside, carrying with me a serpent my hands could not sense, but which instead I felt coursing through me most thoroughly. Like a ray of sunlight made to orbit around a mortal by the power of the gods, its

coils wrapped around me with a sub-
tle warmth that enflamed my mood
and goaded my steps like a spur.
Dreaming of the waves of the sea
where I believed myself imprisoned,
I attempted to renounce Bacchus.
But the god quickly extinguished my
rebelliousness. On the verge of col-
lapsing, I beseeched the ground that
provides respite, when the serpent,
redoubling its attack, struck on my
chest a most ferocious bite. Pain did
not run through my injured side, but
rather a calm and a kind of drowsi-
ness, as if the serpent had dipped its
fangs into Cybele's cup. There arose
in my mind a fire as tranquil as the
embers glowing through the night on

a crude altar erected to the mountain deities. Attentive and at peace like a nymph of Mount Nysa cradling in her arms the infant Bacchus, I lived in the caves until the hour when Aëllo's cry announced the arrival of the mysteries. I stood in the footsteps of this Bacchante who walks before us like Night, when, head turned to summon the dark, she sets off towards the West.

Maurice de Guérin:
One With Nature

BY
GIAN LOMBARDO

ACCORDING TO THE NINETEENTH-CENTURY
publisher and translator G. S. Trébu-
tien, Maurice de Guérin composed
"The Centaur" and "The Bacchante"
after visiting the Museum of Antiq-
uities with him at the Louvre. It was

63

there that de Guérin was inspired by the palpable representations of ancient Greek and Roman deities. On his own he animated through words the spirits of the centaur and the bacchante.

It is easy to see how those visual representations of those creatures animated de Guérin's imagination. He came into this world as the scion of a family with roots in one arm of the nobility that emerged relatively unscathed from the Revolution, being at a far remove from the political and cultural upheaval centered in Paris. His home was the Chateau le Cayla in Andillac, a small village in the south of France, located near the Pyrenees. There he was born in 1810 and raised in his family's diminutive castle in rural France.

His bucolic life at Cayla was disturbed by the death of his mother in 1819. His older sister, Eugénie, who also became a noted writer, raised the young boy. Both of them had a close relationship throughout de Guérin's life. Groomed by his family to become a priest, he entered a seminary in Toulouse at twelve years old. In 1824 he furthered his studies at Stanislas College, a private Catholic school in Paris.

De Guérin, however, while a deeply spiritual individual, resisted the priesthood. His desire was to write. Yet no one wanted to publish his efforts at essays and journalism. He also wrote poems and sketches, and recorded his observations, which turned into his journal, *Le Cahier vert (The Green Notebook)*, which he started in 1832, when he joined the Abbé Félicité de Lamennais's community La Chênaie, at an estate in Brittany. He stayed at La Chênaie through that winter, absorbing Lamennais's take on Catholicism, which was at odds with both the French clerics and the Vatican. Lamennais's beliefs laid the groundwork for the subsequent development of socialist and democratic Catholicism. In late summer 1833, de Guérin decided to join Lamennais's religious order.

However, this passage into religion was short lived. At the directive of the pope, Lamennais dissolved the community at La Chênaie and his religious order. De Guérin then joined a more traditional and rigid order. By that fall, Maurice fled that staid order and spent the winter of 1833 with one of Lamennais's friends, the poet Hippolyte de la Morvonnais, at an idyllic spot on the Brittany coast. The arc of de Guérin's spirituality resided not in man-made churches and seminaries, but in the wilds of nature.

By the fall of 1834 he had secured a teaching appointment at his former school, Stanislas College, and returned to Paris. There, he fell in with an old college classmate, Jules Barbey d'Aurevilly, a prose writer, noted atheist and dandy. The years 1835 and 1836 saw de Guérin overextended due to a heavy teaching load to support himself, as well as studying for an advance degree, and writing. It is from this period of frenzied work and living that he composed "The Centaur" and "The Bacchante."

While in Paris he fell in love with the already married Baroness Almaury de Maister, a composer who held her own salon. According to a newspaper report many years later, to distract the poet the Baroness married him off in November 1838 to a woman named Caroline de Gervain, who came from the Dutch East Indies. But de Guérin had contracted the great

Romantics' disease — consumption — the year before, and early on in his marriage it roared out of remission. He was brought home to Chateau le Cayla where he died in July 1839, after coming to terms once again with his Catholic faith.

WHEN MAURICE DE GUÉRIN DIED, HE remained unpublished, and many of his manuscripts scattered with his family and friends. But through de Guérin's travels in social circles in Paris, he came to the attention of the critic Charles Augustin Sainte-Beuve, as well as the writer Georges Sand. It was Sand who selected "The Centaur" and another short poem to appear in *La Revue de*

Deux Mondes in May 1840 as a memorial to him. Yet it was not until 1861 that a standalone collection of de Guérin's letters, journal entries and poems was published, edited by his friend G. S. Trébutien, which included an essay by Sainte-Beuve. This edition included the first publication of "The Bacchante." An expanded edition followed the next year, and the work was first translated into English in 1867.

DE GUÉRIN'S WORK, ESPECIALLY "THE Centaur" and "The Bacchante," is redolent with his reverence for the beauty and divinity of the natural world. His writing makes manifest his exceptional powers of the sensory obversation of nature. The effects of his childhood in the rural south of France, and his formative years as an adult in Brittany, are indelibly etched in these two prose poems. Throughout his whole life de Guérin was inherently spiritual and religious. His Catholicism was inextricably wed to the natural world, not the world of men and man-made things. He bridled against the strictures of rules and dogma. Instead, true salvation resided in the breezes and streams, trees, meadows and mountains. This reverence for the wild deeply disturbed his family, and nothing was more pleasing to them than his reacceptance of a more formal Catholism when he made his return home to die.

"The Centaur" and "The Bacchante" represent de Guérin at his most unrestrictive, reflecting his wildest embrace of the divinely natural world. His identification with the centaur and the bacchante is vivid and tangible. His visits to the Louvre's Museum of Antiquities sparked his imagination to make deep connections invested with his awe of nature, his worship of the free reign of the spirit, and his knowledge of classical Greek and Roman texts. The reader is drawn into the being and lives and the senses of the centaur and the bacchante. The idea of duality plays itself out in both prose poems: calm and frenzy, peaks and valleys, dark and light, and most obviously beast (horse) and man for the centaur.

THIS INTERPLAY OF DUALITY IS ALSO significant, with the form of both pieces being expressed as prose poetry: that duality of prose and poetry. De Guérin could have easily written both pieces in verse. Indeed, there is another piece from that period, the fragment "Glaucus," that was written in verse. However, de Guérin was conscious that the music of verse could distract, and deflect, from the content of the discourse, and from the shape and hew of the images. Despite how dressed the language is, what comes across is the importance of the narrative, the stories of both the centaur and the bacchante, not their song. It is their character and sensibilities that hold sway.

Possibly the work of his good friend Barbey d'Aurevilly, a short story writer, rubbed off on him. (Barbey d'Aurevilly did later in his career dedicate a prose poem to de Guérin.) However, early on, as a pre-adolescent, de Guérin experimented with poetic prose for a prose poem entitled "Sounds of Nature" and a hybrid prose/verse piece called "Ball, Promenade and Dream at Smyrna" so the method of the form was not alien to him.

These two prose poems by de Guérin were being written about the same time as Louis Bertrand was independently writing his *Gaspard de la nuit*. Both de Guérin's and Bertrand's prose poems were published only posthumously. Betrand's *Gaspard* served as the model and inspiration for Charles Baudelaire's *Paris Spleen* (also published posthumously). And Trébutien's edition of de Guérin's work did appear during the period when Baudelaire was composing *Paris Spleen*. While the approaches are greatly different (de Guérin uses a sustained and charged narrative that carries its poetic weight both in cadence and content that is almost symphonic, while Bertrand uses crystalline bursts of language to fashion quick portraits and sketches), both poets endeavor to extend the boundaries of achieving poetic effects. There is a conscious abandonment of the line and stanza and the overtly musical, and the concomitant embrace of the poetic potential of the sentence and paragraph, with the undulations of the cadences of prose.

When looking at the lineage of the prose poem it is far plainer to see the movement from Bertrand to Baudelaire and Rimbaud and Mallarmé, and from the latter three poets it is easier to make connection to the prose poem in English. Our connection with de Guérin is far less transparent. There might be strains of "The Centaur" and "The Bacchante" in Lautréamont's *Les chants de Maldoror* or even in Huysmans *Au rebours*, but the path becomes overgrown with brambles and vines. On the whole, "The Centaur" and "The Bacchante" provide the aura of singularities and are not easy reads. The diction, and complex grammatical and syntactical constructions, can make reading, and translating, the pieces labyrinthine at best. Faithfully adhering to de Guérin's language and style can result in a ponderously and pompously unreadable text. One challenge is to make both the centaur and the bacchante come alive as they unfold their lives in de Guérin's highly unique poetic idiom. Another challenge is to bring out the beauty in these texts, and to demonstrate the suppleness of another approach to the prose poem that has been there all this time.

quale [kwa-lay], _Eng_ n 1. A property (such as hardness) considered apart from things that have that property. 2. A property that is experienced as distinct from any source it may have in a physical object. _Ital._ pron.a. 1. Which, what. 2. Who. 3. Some. 4. As, just as.

CPSIA information can be obtained
at www.ICGtesting.com
Printed in the USA
BVHW080751260821
615084BV00002B/74